PRAYERS FOR ORDINARY TIME

PRAYERS FOR ORDINARY TIME

JUST IN TIME!

Abingdon Press
Nashville

JUST IN TIME!
PRAYERS FOR ORDINARY TIME

Copyright © 2012 by Abingdon Press

All rights reserved.

This book is printed on acid-free paper.

ISBN 978-1-4267-5478-4

12 13 14 15 16 17 18 19 20 21—10 9 8 7 6 5 4 3 2 1

MANUFACTURED IN THE UNITED STATES OF AMERICA

CONTENTS

Contents

INTRODUCTION

Christians see time as redemptive. Our journey through the year brings us time and again to the great cycles of Advent/Christmas/Epiphany and Lent/Easter/Pentecost. Each year we encounter in these seasons God's great acts in history: the mystery of the Incarnation, the drama of the Passion, the miracle of Resurrection, the birth of the church. Small wonder, then, that we sometimes reach the end of these cycles and feel a sense of letdown, of moving from the extraordinary to the *ordinary*.

But if we believe, as Christian faith teaches us, that God is the Lord of time, then all our days and moments are shot through with the presence of the divine. In the season we call in English "ordinary time," we remember, celebrate, and anticipate all of God's many works, from creation's dawn to history's consummation. In ordinary time we are dealing with nothing less than the living God.

The prayers and litanies in this volume reflect that reality. Written with poetic insight and spiritual depth, they will aid all who use them in calling on God's people to lift up their hearts. Written with the common themes of ordinary time in mind, but not tied to specific Sundays within the lectionary cycle, these *Just in Time! Prayers for Ordinary Time* can be used at any point of this essential season of the church year.

—*The Editors*

Sunday 1

Call to Worship

Leader: This morning, O God, hear our voices.

People: This morning, O God, we raise our voices to you.

Leader: Trusting in the abundance of your love, we enter your house.

People: We bow down in awe and worship before you.

Leader: Lead us, O Lord, in your righteousness.

People: Make your ways clear before us.

Opening Prayer

God of mercy and redemption,
  be with us today.
As we gather in this place,
  safe from the storms of life that rage outside,
  be our strength and our refuge.
We open our hearts and minds to you;
  fill them with your joy and your love,
  your peace and your reassurance. Amen.

Prayer of Confession

It is time to confess our humanity before our neighbors
 and before our gracious God.
Let us be true to our best selves as God sees us.
Let us be free to speak the truth in love.
 Turn us once again to our interior lives,
  for we know we need not hide from you.
 Too often, our habits hurt rather than help.
 Heal us, O God.
 Help us to receive love from others
  especially when we least expect it.
 Help us to focus on what we have now,
  rather than what we left behind to follow Jesus.
 When we feel like strangers,
  welcome us into your loving embrace.
 When we try to ignore the stranger,
  give us the courage to reach out
   and to be a friend of Christ to them.
 We ask these things in the name of Jesus,
  who went the distance,
   and found you every step of the way. Amen.

Words of Assurance

There is no wrong
 that God cannot make right.

There is no chasm
   that can separate us
      from God's love.
The Lord is patient and kind,
   generous and good.
God will not forsake you
   or leave you.
Turn to the Lord with confidence
   and put your faith in God's great mercy.
By the power of Jesus Christ,
   we are made whole. Amen.

Unison Prayer

In a world of violence and tumult,
   we turn to you O God.
You are our strength and our protector,
   the source of comfort and peace.
We pray for those who are oppressed.
Defend them with your love,
   and bring them comfort in times of trial.
We pray for the poor and needy,
   whose daily struggles overwhelm them.
Stir up within us a passion for justice
   that we might serve you
      as we work for righteousness.
When warfare threatens the powerless,

3

defend them by your might,
and bring your peace
    to all the nations. Amen.

Benediction

As Jesus calmed the storm,
    Jesus brings us peace today.
Go forth in faith, with hearts of courage,
    to share God's peace with the world.

Sunday 2

Call to Worship

Leader: We come this morning with joy, to worship God.

People: We do not come to justify ourselves.

Leader: For you, O God, do not judge us by our righteous-ness,

People: but you accept us as we are, out of your great love.

Leader: We come with joy to worship you.

People: We come with grateful hearts to worship you.

Opening Prayer

Lord, Lord,
   we call to you in our desire to know you
      and to make your ways our own.
Teach us, take us, transform us,
that we may serve you with our whole selves
   and do the will of our God in heaven.
Lord, Lord,
   be with us now. Amen.

Prayer of Confession

Life-giving God,
   we are filled with fear and doubt.
We worry that we do not have enough.
We are overwhelmed by the world's problems.
We see danger everywhere.
We are blind to your work.
Give us trusting hearts.
Show us life's possibilities.
Heal the world's brokenness.
Use us as agents of change.
Remove our doubt and fear,
   and teach us to live in you. Amen.

Words of Assurance

We long to mend our ways.
Christ can bear these sins
   for all who eagerly wait for him.
His sacrifice on our behalf,
   his grace toward us,
      washes us anew.

Unison Prayer

God of steadfast love,
   we live in a violent world.

Nations are at war.
Families rebel.
People nurture hatred and malice.
We grieve for those lost to violence—
    for the lives cut short,
    for broken relationships,
    for dreams destroyed.
We feel powerless against such great evil.
Come, O God,
    surround us with your presence.
Work within our world
    to nurture tenderness, forgiveness,
    caring, and peace.
Show us your truth.
Redeem us, O Lord. Amen.

Benediction

Christ's touch has healed you.
God's love has restored you.
The Spirit goes with you.
Go in peace to share the joy of God's love.

SUNDAY 3

Call to Worship

Leader: Come worship God!

People: We come gladly to worship God!

Leader: Come worship God in freedom!

People: We come freely, knowing God welcomes us!

Leader: For we are freed of the law's requirement,

People: We are free to trust God's powerful grace.

Leader: We have known the power of grace in our lives.

People: We come thankfully and faithfully to worship!

Opening Prayer

O God, we come into your gracious presence
   preoccupied with our cares,
     afraid to face our emptiness.
Disclose your wisdom
   in the reading of your Holy Word,
     and in the proclamation of your gospel.
May our labors be pleasing to you,
   and may we be inspired to proclaim the good news
      of Jesus our Sovereign. Amen.

Prayer of Confession

Compassionate God,
    we confess that we have failed you.
We have not proclaimed your word.
We have caused others to suffer.
We have been afraid to answer your call.
Forgive us, O God.
Touch us with your Spirit,
    and heal our brokenness.
Give us courage to go where you send us.
Give us wisdom to share your love. Amen.

Words of Assurance

Hear the good news.
God's mercy is plentiful, and God's grace is abundant.
Receive the bread of forgiveness and steadfast love.

Unison Prayer

God of our days,
    you call us to work in your world.
Strengthen our arms
    and encourage our hearts
        for the tasks you lay before us.
Help us to lay aside our worries
    and to rejoice in your gifts.

Silence our conflicts
  and teach us gentleness and mercy.
May all we do, praise you forever. Amen.

Benediction

Children of God,
  go forth dancing, singing, and praising.
Dance joy into sorrowful places!
Sing hope into places of despair!
Praise God this day and always!

Sunday 4

Call to Worship

Leader: Lord, your children are weary.

People: God, give us your rest.

Leader: Your children are hungry.

People: God, give us your food.

Leader: Your children are thirsty.

People: God, give us your holy water.

Leader: Your children are overwhelmed.

People: God, give us your strength.

Leader: Your children are confused.

People: God, give us your wisdom.

Leader: Your children are frightened.

People: God, give us your courage.

Leader: Your children are disheartened.

People: God, give us your inspiration.

Leader: Your children are scattered.

People: God, gather us together, and hold us in your holy, loving arms.

Leader: As a deer pants for streams of water,

People: so our souls pant for you, O God.

Leader: Our souls thirst for the living God.

People: Wet our lips with your living waters, O God.

Leader: To God we open our downcast souls.

People: Refresh us with your love and your songs.

Leader: To God we direct all our hurts and hopes.

People: You are the source of our hope and our salvation.

Opening Prayer

Dear God of possibility, potential, and promise,
     we offer our lives as laborers in your field.
We offer you gifts of financial resources
     from the blessings we have received from you.
May our offerings be a source of healing and wholeness
     to others as well as to ourselves.
Visit us as stranger and as Savior
     that in our living we may laugh, love,
     and proclaim the good news of Christ's coming.
In the name of our Shepherd and our Sovereign, we pray.
Amen.

Prayer of Confession

We can't help ourselves, Lord,
     try as we may,
     we always seem to forget your teachings;
     we always seems to ignore your judgments.

We renounce your word,
  and we fail to follow your commandments.
Our disobedience deserves your punishment,
  yet you have promised us your steadfast love.
Lord, your faithfulness has always proved true,
  your covenant remains constant.
You will never alter your promise to us.
You will never break your word.
Through your name,
  we lift our heads.
And in your name,
  we offer our prayer. Amen.

Words of Assurance

Hear the good news.
God's mercy is plentiful, and God's grace is abundant.
Receive the bread of forgiveness and steadfast love.

Unison Prayer

God, we are your people.
Transform us and make us anew.
Spin us into strong threads
  of love and caring.
Weave us into a community
  of wisdom and compassion,
  kindness and rejoicing.

Sew us into garments
   of strength and dignity.
We are your people,
   the work of your hands.
Let us praise you forever. Amen.

Benediction

Leader: May we go forth, led by God!

People: Lead us, O God, in your righteousness.

Leader: Make your ways clear before us.

People: Guide us in the ways that lead to truth.

Leader: Go with us each step of the way, O God.

People: Be our companion and our guide.

Leader: May we go forth rejoicing,

People: knowing that God goes before us and with us.

Sunday 5

Call to Worship

Leader: Come, be cleansed of all that binds us to our brokenness.

People: We shall be free!

Leader: Cleansed by God, who can hold us in the chains of yesterday's sins?

People: We shall be free!

Leader: Here in the presence of God's flowing grace, we can overcome all fear!

People: We shall be free of our fear and doubt.

Leader: We are invited to know wholeness. Do you so believe?

People: By faith, we will immerse ourselves today in the love of God, a love that leads to our own healing and wholeness!

Leader: Then let us gather in anticipation and great hope. For we shall know a new freedom from our fears and doubts!

People: Let everyone give thanks and praise to our God!
Let everyone praise God for the Spirit of Christ!

Opening Prayer

O God,
> your children call to you,
> for all the things you do.

Hold us close to thee, bounce us on your knee,
> listen to our woes, wipe our runny noses,
> rock us off to sleep, give us comfort when we weep,
> keep us safe from harm, keep us safe and warm.

Your children you adore,
> now and forevermore. Amen.

Prayer of Confession

My sin is against you
> and you alone, Lord.

You have exposed me for what I am.

All day long, I'm tormented by my sin.

You alone can cleanse me.

You alone can put away my shame.

Turn your face from my guilt, Lord.

Give me a new heart.

Give me a truthful spirit.

Keep me in your presence.

Heal my broken heart.

Return the joy of your salvation to me.
Help me remember the elation
   of your deliverance.
Uphold me by your Holy Spirit.
Hear my prayer.
Hear my cry
   in Jesus' name. Amen.

Words of Assurance

Here is proof that God's faithfulness never ends:
   that while we were yet sinners, God sent God's Son,
   Jesus Christ, to shed his blood for our sins,
      that we might not be cast down into the pit,
      but rise with him to everlasting life.

Unison Prayer

God, you are the gardener,
   gently cultivating the soil of our lives,
   giving us water and life.
Thank you for all you give us,
   for your Spirit that nurtures us,
   bring life and strength.
May we bear the fruits of righteousness,
   gentleness, kindness, and peace.
May we be gentle and forgiving,
   turning away from anger,

working for peace,
rejoicing in each other's gifts. Amen.

Benediction

May the God who is revealed, not in the ferocious wind, not in the earthquake, or even the fire, but in a hushed whisper be with you, comfort you, feed you, and commission you for mighty deeds.

Sunday 6

Call to Worship

Leader: I will exalt you, O Lord!

People: For you lifted me out of the depths!

Leader: O Lord my God, I called to you for help,

People: and you healed me!

Leader: Sing to the Lord, you saints; praise God's holy name.

People: For God's anger lasts only a moment, but the Lord's favor lasts a lifetime.

Leader: Hear, O Lord, and be merciful to me.

People: You turned my wailing into dancing!

Leader: You removed my sackcloth, and clothed me with joy!

People: My heart will sing to you and not be silent.

Leader: O Lord, my God, I will give you thanks forever!

People: O Lord, my God, I will give you thanks forever!

Opening Prayer

God of love,
  you peer into each soul and heart

and cherish us just the same.
Be with us now as we come into your presence
    with reverence and humility,
    with joy and expectation.
Help us to live more fully
    with the realization of your endless love for us.
Teach us to live and love as a family.
Guide us to be good children,
        as you are our perfect parent. Amen.

Prayer of Confession

Though we labor for food that perishes, Lord,
    you will give us bread that endures forever.
Though we do what displeases you—
    you will show us mercy;
    you will forgive our sin.
Though the truth
    may be hidden in darkness, Lord,
    you will teach us wisdom.
Teach us; feed us; forgive us. Amen.

Words of Assurance

Do not be distressed or angry with yourselves,
    for the God who reconciled Joseph and his brothers,
        can surely reconcile us.
God's mercy extends to everyone.
Rejoice and live in unity!

Unison Prayer

We give thanks with one voice
   to our great high priest,
      the Lord Jesus Christ. Amen.

Benediction

Leader: Do not grow weary of doing good!

People: We go forth now to carry the burdens of one another.

Leader: To the glory of God, let us walk in the Spirit of freedom.

People: We go forth to live, and to offer to all, the freedom we know in Christ.

Leader: Be changed and know the joy of new beginnings!

People: We go forth in joy and laughter, to serve the world, and bring the kingdom of God to earth.

Sunday 7

Call to Worship

Leader: God calls us to judge with justice.

People: We will judge justly.

Leader: God calls us to show no partiality to the wicked.

People: We will do what is right in God's sight.

Leader: God calls us to rescue the weak and the needy.

People: We will deliver them from the hand of the wicked.

Leader: By living God's justice and mercy

People: we shall be spared the judgment of God.

Opening Prayer

Be with us, O God,
    and be gracious with your needy servants.
To you we bring the cares of our lives,
    the deepest yearnings of our souls.
Strengthen us, we pray,
    by the healing balm of your love
    and the steadfast guidance of your teachings.

We lift up our hands
    and open our hearts
        to embrace your transforming love. Amen.

Prayer of Confession

God of steadfast love,
    we so often fail you.
We nurture anger and violence,
    and fail to see that all people
        are your beloved children.
Our words are destructive
    and hurtful.
Teach us to imitate you.
May love and kindness
    spring up in our lives.
May we be tenderhearted
    and forgiving.
May our words bring healing
    and reconciliation. Amen.

Words of Assurance

In all things, at all times, and in all places,
    you are forgiven.
The One who gave us life also sent us Christ,
    that by his sacrifice on the cross
        we are cleansed of all failings.

Claim this grace as your own
   and go forward in joy. Amen.

Unison Prayer

Teach us, Jesus,
   to live as servants.
Teach us Jesus,
   to serve each other.
Teach us Jesus,
   to abide in your ways—
         in humility and meekness,
         with compassion and empathy,
         without pride or boastfulness,
            and with a smile.
Teach us to do unto others,
   as if we were doing unto you. Amen.

Benediction

Leader: God calls: "Go where I send you."
People: God will show us the way.
Leader: God calls: "Go where I send you."
People: God will bless us.
Leader: God calls: "Go where I send you."
People: God will bless all the earth.

Sunday 8

Call to Worship

Leader: O God, a teenager dies from a stray bullet.

People: A child is assaulted by an angry father.

Leader: A mother buys drugs for herself instead of milk for
her children.

People: An abandoned infant cries for a warm embrace.

Leader: Cries go unheard.

People: Needs go unanswered.

Leader: Pain goes untreated.

People: Touch our hearts, O Lord.

Leader: Warm our souls.

People: Guide our steps.

Leader: Move us to love your children,

People: as much as we love ourselves.

Opening Prayer

Welcoming God,
We come to you as we are,
seeking approval,

seeking forgiveness,

seeking to find our way home.

Help us welcome others,

as we would like to be welcomed.

Teach us to value the rewards that come

from a life of servanthood.

Help us embrace the cost of discipleship,

that we may be welcomed into your eternal home.

Amen.

Prayer of Confession

God does not demand blood sacrifice from us.

Expect God to be merciful.

Let us speak these words of confession in one voice,

that God's promise of mercy

may be fulfilled in our prayer.

Hear us now, O God of great wisdom and understanding.

In this house of prayer,

we thank you for your gracious leading.

We confess that it is a challenge

to know how to live as followers of Jesus.

We struggle sometimes.

When we are fearful or uncertain,

give us wisdom.

When we are defensive or even hostile

to interruptions and opportunities,

give us clarity and understanding.
When we act as if we lack what we need,
    forgive us and inspire us with your Holy Presence.
We pray in the name of the One
    who came to bring life and spirit to this world.
Amen.

Words of Assurance

Hear the good news:
what we do matters,
but our salvation is God's doing.
God hears our complaints,
but also our prayers.
God will not forget us.
In Christ's name, we are forgiven. Amen.

Unison Prayer

Leader: See, the home of God is among mortals.
         God will dwell with them
            and they will be a holy people.
         God will be with them
            and will wipe away every tear from their
            eyes.
Death will be no more.
Mourning and crying and pain will be no more,
         for the first things have passed away.

People: **Almighty God,**
you have chosen to dwell with us
and through your presence,
you transform the world.
Teach us how to live in your kingdom,
that we may put away former ways of death
and dwell in peace with all people
in your holy presence. Amen.

Benediction

Share with all the world
the love you have received this day.
Take the blessing of the Creator,
the grace of the Redeemer,
and the love of the Sustainer
as you leave this place. Amen.

Sunday 9

Call to Worship

Leader: Our hearts are hungry.

People: We seek to hear your word.

Leader: We wander from sea to sea, but we do not hear.

People: We run to and fro, but we do not find the word we seek.

Leader: Come to this quiet place; center your hearts.

People: We will hear the word of the Lord.

Opening Prayer

Merciful God,
  we go through life feeling tested.
Whenever anything goes wrong,
  we wonder,
      what have I done to deserve this?
Help us remember that you seek our salvation,
  not our pain.
Remind us that your ways lead to life,
  not death.

Teach us again that you are holy and just,
    abiding in steadfast love,
    that we might rise above our doubts
        and embrace your mercy. Amen.

Prayer of Confession

O God,
    we come with sighs too deep for words.
We find ourselves at times too self-centered.
We show partiality to those who are like us.
We fear and reject those who are foreign to us.
We close our ears to their cries
    and our hearts to their needs.
We do not even offer crumbs.
Help us to have a generous and open spirit.
May we always be willing to admit our mistakes
    in judgment and in deed
        and work to correct the injustices they may cause.
May we have a living faith
    and transform us with your radical love,
        that we may be the people you call us to be. Amen.

Words of Assurance

Do not worry; the Lord is near.
God hears our prayers with compassion
    and with abundant, steadfast love.
Rejoice, for in the name of Jesus Christ, we are forgiven!

Unison Prayer

Gracious Father,
   we join together in songs of praise,
   raising our voices in joyful anticipation
      of your victory in the world.
There is no Rock,
   no holy one besides you.
You are as solid as a mountain,
   as faithful as a mother,
      and bring justice down like a king.
We thank you for the gift of your Son,
   who cleanses us in mind, body, and spirit.
May we walk in your ways,
   and guide each other along the path. Amen.

Benediction

As a gentle father,
   God has opened his hand
      and blessed us with his touch.
As a loving mother,
   God has wiped away our tears
      and healed our every hurt.
Let us leave this place now
   satisfied in his embrace.

Sunday 10

Call to Worship

Leader: Like green olive trees, growing in the house of the Lord,

People: we flourish in God's presence.

Leader: Let us trust the steadfast love of the Lord

People: forever and ever.

Leader: Let us thank the Lord

People: forever and ever.

Leader: Let us proclaim the name of our God.

People: We declare God's steadfast love.

Opening Prayer

God of wisdom and mercy,

In your kingdom, the lowly are made great

   as they wait upon you and receive your grace.

Open our hearts to this kingdom today.

Renew in us a childlike faith,

   as we hear your word and sing your praises,

that we might go from this place
    proclaiming the good news of the gospel. Amen.

Prayer of Confession

Holy God,
    there is something about connecting with those we love,
    the sense of something holding us together—
    invisible strings, silent songs echoing back and forth;
    one cord, with one person on each end.
But when disagreement creeps in
    and we enter into conflict—
        how the ropes tighten;
        how the notes become strained.
We are tempted to cut the ribbons that bind us together.
Help us remember that we are created
    to reflect your image.
Help us recall that the reward comes from holding on—
    from saying to others,
    "I am not like you, but I am with you";
    "I do not agree with you, but I am still here,
        connected to you."
God of Conflict, God of Reconciliation,
    prepare us for the discomfort of disagreement.
Let us hold fast to the ties that bind us together.
In our anxiety, let us twist and adjust,
    but give us the endurance to never let go. Amen.

Words of Assurance

Hear the witness of scripture:
God listens; God helps. Now is the day of salvation.
Open wide your hearts and receive God's forgiveness.
Amen.

Unison Prayer

Loving God, who can hide from your presence? Who else
knows us or loves us so well? Keep on loving us, O God, and
free us from all that keeps us from true intimacy with you,
and with others. Heal our brokenness, and restore us to the
wholeness for which we were intended. Through the vast-
ness of your love, we are with you to the end. Amen.

Benediction

Wherever you may be,
   may you see the gates of heaven.
Wherever you may be,
   may you find the wheat among the weeds.
Wherever you may be,
   may you turn stone pillows into pillars of God.
Go with eyes and hearts wide open
   to God's lively presence!
Go in peace and hope!

SUNDAY 11

Call to Worship

Leader: Jesus Christ is the image of the invisible God, the firstborn of all creation.

People: **All things were created through and for the Word made flesh.**

Leader: Jesus is the head of the body, the church.

People: **Jesus is the beginning, the firstborn from the dead.**

Leader: In Christ, the fullness of God was pleased to dwell.

People: **Through Christ, God is at work in the world, reconciling all things.**

Leader: Come as a reconciled and holy people.

People: **Worship Jesus Christ, our hope and glory.**

Opening Prayer

God of wisdom,
   let your word fall upon us this day.
Let your law of love embed itself in our hearts.

Let your grace and mercy take root in our lives.
Open our hearts to your nurture,
   that we may grow in faith.
Open our lives to your guidance,
   that we may grow in service.
Send your Holy Spirit upon us,
   that we may become true disciples of Jesus Christ.
Amen.

Prayer of Confession

Most merciful God,
   Jesus teaches us that it is more difficult
      for a wealthy person to enter your kingdom,
      than it is for a camel to go through the eye
      of a needle.
Too often we have been blinded by the glitter of gold
   and sought to acquire more money and possessions
      than we need.
In our selfishness, we have ignored your call
   to share our bounty with the poor in our midst,
   choosing instead to walk away from the needy
      in guilty sadness.
We beg your mercy and forgiveness.
We await your strength
   and guidance to do better. Amen.

Words of Assurance

There is forgiveness and healing with God.
God's steadfast love
  has the power to redeem our brokenness
    and make us whole.

Unison Prayer

Gracious Lord,
  help us trust your goodness and gentle humility,
  that we might bring our failings before you.
In our weakness, grant us the certainty
  that we are made strong by relying on Christ,
  who is our truth and our salvation. Amen.

Benediction

You have been fed with the bread of heaven,
and blessed by the presence and peace of God.
Now go into the world in the peace of Christ
to be bread for the world.
  We go in Christ's name. Amen.

Sunday 12

Call to Worship

Leader: The earth and its people call out for healing.

People: Restore us again, O God of our salvation.

Leader: The skies cry out to blow clean once again.

People: Restore us again, O God of our salvation.

Leader: Hallowed be your name, O God.

People: May your kingdom come! May your will be done, on earth as it is in heaven.

Opening Prayer

Gracious God,
   open our hearts to your word this day.
Light our paths
   with the brightness of your love and wisdom.
Guide us as we seek to walk in your ways
   and grow in your truth.
Accept our offerings of praise,
   that our songs and our words may be transformed
      into your songs and your words.
In Christ's name, we pray. Amen.

Prayer of Confession

It is time to confess our humanity before our neighbors
    and before our gracious God.
Let us be true to our best selves as God sees us.
Let us be free to speak the truth in love.
    Turn us once again to our interior lives,
        for we know we need not hide from you.
    Too often, our habits hurt rather than help.
    Heal us, O God.
    Help us to receive love from others
        especially when we least expect it.
    Help us to focus on what we have now,
        rather than what we left behind to follow Jesus.
    When we feel like strangers,
        welcome us into your loving embrace.
    When we try to ignore the stranger,
        give us the courage to reach out
            and to be a friend of Christ to them.
    We ask these things in the name of Jesus,
        who went the distance,
            and found you every step of the way. Amen.

Words of Assurance

Leader: We belong to the King of glory who joyfully sets
          us free.
Leader: In Christ's healing hands, you find forgiveness.

People: In Christ's healing touch, you find forgiveness.
People: Glory be to God! Amen.

Unison Prayer

Eternal God,
   when others see your love for us
   and how we are set apart,
   they often do not speak peaceably to us.
When others hear the dreams
   you have planted within us,
   they often cannot speak peaceably to us.
When others experience
   how you transform our misfortunes
   into works for good,
   they often will not speak peaceably to us.
But we pray someday that they will speak peace
   and be restored in love.
Make us beautiful and humble, God,
   to bear the good news of your peace. Amen.

Benediction

May the God of Jacob, Joseph, Reuben, and Judah;
   Peter, James, John, and Andrew;
   Mary, Martha, Ruth, and Lydia,
      grant you grace to abide in God's love,
      give you peace to abide in God's forgiveness,
      and the power to live in God's faithfulness. Amen.

SUNDAY 13

Call to Worship

Leader: Winds blow, storms rage.

People: God is our refuge.

Leader: Floods rise, waves batter.

People: God is our refuge.

Leader: Wars ravage, violence threatens.

People: God is our refuge.

Leader: Corruption rules, greed reigns.

People: God is our refuge.

Leader: We cry to God; God hears us.

People: God is our refuge.

Leader: We are safe; we are warm.

People: Thanks be to God.

Opening Prayer

Our gracious and ever loving God,
    we come in the midst of summer
        looking for refreshment.
We rest in the knowledge
    of the wonderful works you have done for us,

and of the deep and abiding love you have for us
  and for all God's people.
Search our hearts.
Fill our soul with your indwelling Spirit
  who whispers to our soul
    that all will be well if we but trust in you.
Shine your light before us,
  that we may see our path to you
    and to your kingdom on earth. Amen.

Prayer of Confession

Life-giving God,
  we are filled with fear and doubt.
We worry that we do not have enough.
We are overwhelmed by the world's problems.
We see danger everywhere.
We are blind to your work.
Give us trusting hearts.
Show us life's possibilities.
Heal the world's brokenness.
Use us as agents of change.
Remove our doubt and fear,
  and teach us to live in you. Amen.

Words of Assurance

If we confess our sins, God is faithful and will forgive us.
God provides freely, in the bread of heaven,

all the mercy we need for life everlasting.

The good news is forgiveness in the name of Christ Jesus.

Unison Prayer

Generous God,
>   thank you for all you give us:
>>   a world of beauty and grace,
>>   a community of love and caring,
>>   an opportunity for new life
>>>   through your Son, Jesus Christ.

We pray for all who are in need:
>   for victims of injustice throughout the world,
>   for children who are hungry,
>   for elders who are lonely and long for community,
>   for men who are discouraged,
>   for women who need healing.

Breathe your new life into places of despair,
>   and restore all people
>   to the wholeness of your love.

We offer ourselves as your people,
>   ready to share your love with others. Amen.

Benediction

It is time to take the party to the streets!

Go out to celebrate our common kinship
>   as children of God.

Go out to tell the good news of Christ
  to every sister and brother.
Go out to let the power of the Holy Spirit
  unite us around the world.
Go out to continue this family reunion
  with all those who are longing to join the party.
Go out and rejoice!

Sunday 14

Call to Worship

Leader: Come, let us remember the graciousness of God.

People: The gospel is the power of God for salvation!

Leader: Let us remember the graciousness of God.

People: We are redeemed through the sacrifice of Christ Jesus.

Leader: Let us remember the graciousness of God.

People: We rejoice in God's generous gift of life.

Leader: Let us remember the graciousness of God.

Opening Prayer

God, make known to us all you have done,
   and all you have yet to do.
Speak to us once more
   your powerful message of deliverance—
         deliverance from oppression and injustice,
         deliverance from fear and hopelessness,
         deliverance from slavery to sin and death.
Free us in this hour from all that would stifle our spirits.

May your word in us bear fruit for all the world.
Amen.

Prayer of Confession

Compassionate God,
    we confess that we have failed you.
We have not proclaimed your word.
We have caused others to suffer.
We have been afraid to answer your call.
Forgive us, O God.
Touch us with your Spirit,
    and heal our brokenness.
Give us courage to go where you send us.
Give us wisdom to share your love. Amen.

Words of Assurance

The Lord is gracious to us and gentle.
The Lord heals our souls with love.
The Lord is merciful,
    providing spiritual food for the hungry.
Be healed in your hearts and be fed in your souls
    by the forgiveness found in Jesus Christ our Lord.

Unison Prayer

Your love comforts us,
    God of our lives.

In the midst of our rebellion,
    you love us still.
Your love also frightens us:
    calling us to be bold;
    calling us to walk into places of power
        and speak your truth;
    calling us to weep without shame,
        in deep love and longing;
    calling us to live anew in the life of Christ.
With your comfort, make us whole.
But do not stop challenging us,
    even when we are fearful and timid. Amen.

Benediction

Hear these words of exhortation:
    to save your life you must lose it,
    and in losing your life in Christ,
        you will find life everlasting.
Recognize the stumbling blocks in your life,
    and recall the example of Moses,
    who recognized the voice of God
        calling from the burning bush.
By these examples, go with the assurance
    that I AM WHO I AM will be with you,
        now and forever.

Sunday 15

Call to Worship

Leader: Come, friends in Christ, let us worship at the throne of God.

People: We are here to receive God's grace.

Leader: Come, friends in Christ,

People: let us worship at the foot of the cross.

Leader: We are here to grow stronger in our faith in Christ Jesus.

People: Come, friends in Christ, let us worship with hopeful hearts.

Leader: We will worship in spirit and in truth.

Opening Prayer

Gracious God of the universe,
   you have called us here from different walks of life.
From our diverse backgrounds,
   you have knit us into a unified family of faith.
We pray that, even as you have accepted us as we are,
   we can learn to accept others

whose ways are different from our own.
As we open our hearts to you,
  show us the way to open our hearts to others.
In your presence today, O God,
  may we worship together without exclusion
      and rejoice together without ceasing. Amen.

Prayer of Confession

Surprising God,
  we often look for you
      in all the wrong places.
      We work hard on huge anthems of intricate praise,
and we forget to seek you
  in the simple melody of a child.
      We craft elaborate pageants full of drama,
and we forget to seek you
  in the unrehearsed cry of the heart.
We work to build the best programs,
  the most successful classes,
  the most sought-after workshops,
      and we forget to seek you
          in the eyes of the lonely woman
              at the bus stop.
Guide us, O God,
  and open our hearts to find you
      in the unexpected places of our lives.

This we pray in the name of the One who came,
  not as a king, but as a carpenter. Amen.

Words of Assurance

God's word has the power to save your soul.
God has anointed you with gladness.
You are forgiven to live in joy.

Unison Prayer

Leader: Lord God, we have come to hear you speak to our hearts. Yet there is much that binds us and blunts our hearing. As your daughters and sons, we appeal to you for healing and liberation—
People: **set us free!**
Leader: From cancer, AIDS, and heart disease—
People: **set us free!**
Leader: From diabetes, Alzheimer's, and Parkinson's—
People: **set us free!**
Leader: From multiple sclerosis, birth defects, chemical dependency, and depression—
People: **set us free!**
Leader: Through modern medicine and the miracles of science—
People: **set us free!**
Leader: Through your healing touch, bless our lives, as only you can bless—
People: **set us free! Amen.**

Benediction

Stand firm in the spirit;
   strive side by side;
    and live in a manner worthy
       of the gospel of Christ.
Go in peace. Amen.

SUNDAY 16

Call to Worship

Leader: Jesus has called us to proclaim the good news of God's redeeming love.

People: **We come to worship as people who have heard and responded to God's call in Jesus Christ.**

Leader: Jesus has called us to heal the nations and bring hope to all we meet.

People: **We come from all races and cultures to be Christ's disciples.**

Leader: Jesus has called us to demonstrate compassion and commitment.

People: **We come as disciples to worship and gain strength for our journey. Let us worship God together. Alleluia!**

Opening Prayer

Our most gracious God,
    we humbly enter your presence this morning.
In our brokenness,

we may feel unworthy to be called your children,
yet we rejoice knowing that you have chosen us
    to be your own.
We feel the warmth of your embrace as you gather us.
Though once separated from you through sin,
   you have reconciled us into a family
      through your forgiveness and mercy.
Help us to be a reflection of your acceptance and grace.
In the name of Christ, our Savior, we pray. Amen.

Prayer of Confession

Leader: Merciful God, you called us for freedom in Christ,
but we have submitted to sin's yoke of slavery.

People: Have mercy upon us.

Leader: We have misused our freedom, making it an
opportunity for self-indulgence instead of loving
our neighbors as ourselves.

People: Have mercy upon us.

Leader: We have been jealous, angry, quarrelsome,
impure, and idolatrous.

People: Have mercy upon us.

Words of Assurance

Our God is always ready
   to rain blessings on us,
     to pour hope into our souls.

By the life and love of Jesus the Christ,
we are redeemed in God's eyes.

Unison Prayer

God of blessing,
you call us to venture into the unknown
and trust that you know the way.
We are often afraid,
reluctant to answer you,
hesitant to take the risks.
Give us the faith to overcome our fears.
Remind us of your power to sustain us
when we are weak.
Heal what is broken
and bring us back to life.
May we live in the midst of your blessings,
ever rejoicing in your love. Amen.

Benediction

Leader: This is a day of new beginnings.
People: This is our day of victory.
Leader: The Lord has taken us from our time of trouble,
People: and given us new life in the midst of trial.
Leader: Some say bigger is better, age equals wisdom, and
the race is won only by the swift.

People: **But God says, I will give the victory to those who call on my name.**

Leader: O God, we shout for joy over the victories you work in our lives.

People: **This is our day of victory!**

Sunday 17

Call to Worship

Leader: We gather together as family.

People: God is our heavenly parent.

Leader: We gather united as brothers and sisters.

People: God is our heavenly parent.

Leader: We gather to praise and worship in gladness.

People: God is our heavenly parent.

Leader: We gather to sing hymns of thanksgiving.

People: God is our heavenly parent.

Leader: We gather to raise up prayers and petitions.

People: God is our heavenly parent.

Leader: And we gather to listen to God's loving voice.

People: God is our heavenly parent.

Opening Prayer

O Lord, our Lord,
   how majestic is your name in all the earth!
We come before you today
   seeking freedom from our selfishness and limited views
      of faith and service.

Deliver us from the kind of thinking
    that excludes ourselves
        from your works of salvation and healing.
Speak to us today,
    as you did to Moses from the burning bush,
    and let us know your strength to fulfill the ministry
        you give to us. Amen.

Prayer of Confession

Almighty God,
    you desire health and wholeness
        for all your creation.
Forgive us when we stay trapped
    in unhealthy ways.
Forgive us when we cling
    to our old familiar dis-ease.
Forgive us when we convince ourselves
    that we know better than you.
Help us trust your love and your Spirit
    to lead us on the path of new life.
In Jesus' name we pray. Amen.

Words of Assurance

When we come before God in humility and honesty,
    God draws near to us with forgiveness
        and renewed blessing.
Thanks be to God!

Unison Prayer

In the adventure of life,
  we have found you.
By your powerful grace,
  you have found us.
As we proclaim your mighty deeds,
  we celebrate your justice. Amen.

Benediction

As Jesus calmed the storm,
  Jesus brings us peace today.
Go forth in faith, with hearts of courage,
  to share God's peace with the world.

Sunday 18

Call to Worship

Leader: Today we recall what God has done:

People: Proclaim it from the housetops.

Leader: God's saving work in Jesus Christ,

People: Proclaim it from the housetops.

Leader: Resurrecting us into new life,

People: Proclaim it from the housetops.

Leader: Releasing us from the power of sin and death,

People: Proclaim it from the housetops.

Leader: Alive to God forevermore.

People: We tell it in the light.

Opening Prayer

God of all seasons,
  come to us anew on this Sunday morning.
As we feel the changing pace of our common lives,
  let us know again the wonder of your ordered world
    and your wonderful desires for our fulfillment.
We come before you with both anxiety and hope.

As we sing and pray,
remove our fears and insecurities
and give us the assurance of things hoped for,
the evidence of things not seen. Amen.

Prayer of Confession

You stand beside a wall
with a plumb line in your hand, Lord—
the wall that I have built.
What once was a straight, strong wall of protection,
a sanctuary against all that might harm me,
is now revealed as a bowed, bulging,
weak wall of separation
that I have used to conceal myself
within a dark prison of my own making.
I know that your perfect judgment
finds me wanting.
Free me, Lord;
I am my own worst enemy.
Level my feeble fortress,
and rebuild me in the strength of your love
and your forgiveness.
Lead me from my darkness
into your light. Amen.

Words of Assurance

There is no wrong
that God cannot make right.

There is no chasm
   that can separate us
      from God's love.
The Lord is patient and kind,
   generous and good.
God will not forsake you
   or leave you.
Turn to the Lord with confidence
   and put your faith in God's great mercy.
By the power of Jesus Christ,
   we are made whole. Amen.

Unison Prayer

God of grace and mercy,
   whether we are lifelong laborers,
   or new arrivals in your vineyard,
      we know you value us just as we are.
Hear now the prayers of thanks and concern
   that we now speak aloud
      or raise silently from our hearts.
(Petitions may be offered.)
God of the last, God of the first,
   God of all those in between,
   hear these concerns
      as we seek your presence in our lives
         and in a world in need. Amen.

Benediction

The Lord gives strength to the powerless,
   courage to the fearful,
   faith to the doubting,
   and peace to those who are afraid.
The Lord is our stronghold.
We are safe. Go in peace.

Sunday 19

Call to Worship

Leader: Let those who seek to please God with their goodness hear the good news.

People: Christ will be our goodness!

Leader: Let those who are burdened with guilt for their failures hear the good news.

People: Christ will accomplish all for us and quiet our hearts!

Leader: Take up the discipline of grace.

People: We will embrace the disciplines that empowers us to live as God intends!

Leader: Learn the ways of Christ.

People: The Lord will not condemn us but will fill our souls with peace!

Opening Prayer

Lord, there is no rock like you!
From you, living water flows like a river
through the desert of our souls,

73

bringing life to a parched and thirsty land.
Lord, there is no food that we can eat like yours.
Every word from your mouth is like bread from heaven!
You have spread your table before us.
Fill our cups with your water of life,
   and satisfy our hunger with Christ,
      the living bread, in whose name we pray. Amen.

Prayer of Confession

We long to mend our ways.
Christ can bear these sins
   for all who eagerly wait for him.
His sacrifice on our behalf,
   his grace toward us,
      washes us anew.

Words of Assurance

Loving and merciful Lord,
   by your word we are nourished,
   by your hand we are fed.
Turn our hearts to you now,
   as we lift our prayers to you. Amen.

Unison Prayer

God transforms the weak and fearful.
God gives us power and might.

Declare God's deeds among the peoples.
Share God's peace with the world.

Benediction

As we leave one another and this holy place,
may we be surrounded by the love of God
like a comforting embrace.
May we be protected by the gracious presence
of your Holy Spirit like a warm breeze.
May we be enlightened by the mind of Christ
to seek the shadow and the light.
Go with goodness and with grace
as God's beloved people.
Go in peace. Amen.

Sunday 20

Call to Worship

You care for your people, Lord.
In the heat of the day,
   as we labor in your vineyard,
   we are covered like a cloud by your Holy Spirit.
In the dark of night,
   your fire gives us light and warmth,
   and illuminates our path.
When life's adversities well up before us
   like a great impassable sea,
   you part the angry waters
      and make us walk on solid ground.
We hunger and we thirst,
   yet you never fail to sustain us.
We are overwhelmed by your amazing love.
We humbly offer our thanks through Jesus Christ,
   in whose name we pray. Amen.

Opening Prayer

In times of difference and division,
    save us from rancor and meanness, O God.
Help us focus ourselves on things
    that are excellent and worthy.
Make us witnesses to your way of justice
    and righteousness.
Transform us and transform the world, we pray. Amen.

Prayer of Confession

In times of difference and division,
    save us from rancor and meanness, O God.
Help us focus ourselves on things
    that are excellent and worthy.
Make us witnesses to your way of justice
    and righteousness.
Transform us and transform the world, we pray. Amen.

Words of Assurance

Sisters and brothers,
    Jesus said to the woman with the alabaster jar,
        "Your sins are forgiven."
Hear his words for yourselves,
    and take them into your heart and soul.

Unison Prayer

Holy God, you care for us as a loving parent,
  that we might do the same for others.
Help us so proclaim and bear witness to the gospel,
  that all might recognize your word.
Strengthen us to be pure, upright
  and blameless before others,
that nothing may hinder your teachings.
  In our churches, may the word be taught.
  In our lives, may the word be seen.
  In our hearts, may the word dwell forever. Amen.

Benediction

And now, sisters and brothers,
  go from this place knowing that the God who made you
    also sustains you.
The God who calls you also goes with you.
The God who loved you before you were born
  still loves you today, and into all the tomorrows. Amen.

SUNDAY 21

Call to Worship

Leader: Holy, holy, holy is the Lord of hosts.

People: God, the whole earth is full of your glory!

Leader: We come to praise and exalt the name of the Lord.

People: O God, the whole earth is full of your glory!

Leader: Let us put aside our cares to worship the Lord.

People: O God, the whole earth is full of your glory!

Leader: Glory to God in the highest!

People: O God, the whole earth is full of your glory!

Opening Prayer

Lord of hope and strength, be with us this day as we strive to follow you. May our faith be as deep as the sea—deep enough to carry us to peaceful shores. Nurture us in your love, and guide us with your grace. In Christ's name we pray. Amen.

Prayer of Confession

Ever present One,
   you call us to be your presence,

81

your body in this world,
but too often we get caught up
in being a hand or a foot,
and lose sight of the overarching mission
you set before us.
We fracture into pieces.
We go our separate ways,
forgetting we need each other to be whole.
You have given us your law to be our guide,
but we turn our backs
on what we see as rules and restrictions,
fearful that we will not live up to your expectations.
Help us see with new eyes,
and hear with the ears of our heart,
the liberating spirit of the law
that strengthens and revives and enables us
to be and do all you call us to be and do.
O God of liberation and justice,
help us be faithful witnesses
to your law of love and unity. Amen.

Words of Assurance

Children of God, in humility and gentleness,
Christ came to forgive you and renew your life.
You have been rescued from the power of sin
by the Lord Jesus Christ.

Let your hearts be content and your witness made bold
as you walk in the freedom of God's grace.

Unison Prayer

Loving God, Creator of opportunity and choice,
Giver of justice and mercy,
we pray that our choices
might reflect our life in you.
Where we have sinned,
lead us to repentance.
Where we have repented,
help us to acknowledge your mercy.
Where we have accepted your mercy,
free us to pass it on to others.
We worship you in the name of Jesus Christ
who embodied your justice and love.
Amen.

Benediction

Leader: May the God of hope and strength go with us
today.

People: We feel your love, O Lord.

Leader: May the amazing grace of Christ inspire our
journeys.

People: We know your grace, O Lord.

Leader: We hear the voice of the Lord saying, "Whom shall I send?"

People: We hear your voice, O Lord.

Leader: We long to say with Isaiah, "Here am I; send me!"

SUNDAY 22

Call to Worship

Leader: We are gathered at the lakeshore to hear the word of God.

People: Carry us in your boat, O Lord, and teach us.

Leader: We are prepared to cast our nets in faith and love.

People: We yearn to be amazed at our catch and follow Christ today.

Leader: As we worship together, may we feel the breath of God blowing us toward clear skies and bountiful seas.

People: Praise God whose wisdom and grace guide our way.

Opening Prayer

God of the ages,
we give thanks for your steadfast love and faithfulness.
We come to you today with open hearts and open minds,
ready to praise your name.
May our journey together be fruitful
as we continue to seek your purpose for us. Amen.

Prayer of Confession

We are sometimes doubtful, O God,
    that you are in our midst.
This weary, old world groans in pain.
And we humans are too often enslaved
    by fear and suffering.
It's so easy to lose hope.
Search us, O God,
    and know our hearts and thoughts.
If there is any wrong in us,
    lead us in the way everlasting.
And teach us your hope
    that shines even in seemingly hopeless situations.
Amen.

Words of Assurance

Jesus has reconciled you, and presents you blameless, holy, and irreproachable. Continue, securely established and steadfast in the faith.

Unison Prayer

Loving God, who can hide from your presence? Who else knows us or loves us so well? Keep on loving us, O God, and free us from all that keeps us from true intimacy with you, and with others. Heal our brokenness, and restore us to the wholeness for which we were intended. Through the vast-ness of your love, we are with you to the end. Amen.

Benediction

Leader: We go from this place as those who are blessed!

People: We are filled.

We have joy.

We have all we need.

Leader: From this place we go to give, to bear fruit, to love.

People: Our trust, O God, is in you!

Sunday 23

Call to Worship

Leader: Blessed are those who trust in the Lord, whose trust is the Lord.

People: **They shall be like a tree planted by water, sending out its roots by the stream.**

Leader: They shall not fear the heat, nor wither in the sun.

People: **In the year of drought they are not anxious, for their lives do not cease to bear fruit.**

Leader: Come all you who trust in the Lord!

People: **Let us worship!**

Opening Prayer

God of earth and sky, God of all times and places, we have come to this place to be your people. You have called to us, and we feel a deep longing to know you, to hear you speak to us, to be your church. Just as you revealed your glory to the prophet Moses, as he stood on the mountaintop to receive the Ten Commandments, your glory was seen anew when Jesus stood transfigured before his disciples on the mountaintop. May we not be blinded by your light, but be strengthened by it. With your help, may we see and hear what you have to say to us. Through the power of your Holy Spirit, and by the presence of Christ with us, open our eyes and ears and hearts to know the brightness of your glory. Amen.

Prayer of Confession

Gracious God,
    provider of all we need,
        we are often content to rely on our own devices,
        our creativity, our cleverness.
We congratulate ourselves for our accomplishments,
    yet we find that these achievements and acquisitions
        do not fill the deep hunger inside of us.
We long for the Spirit bread you alone can provide.
Forgive us, merciful God.
Help us receive the blessings you offer,
    that we may be your bread for the world—
        blessed, broken for all.

Words of Assurance

God's steadfast love is trustworthy. God hears our cries and forgives our sins, reconciling us in hope and peace.

Unison Prayer

Help us trust your goodness and gentle humility,
that we might bring our failings before you.
In our weakness, grant us the certainty
that we are made strong by relying on Christ,
who is our truth and our salvation. Amen.

Benediction

Leader: May the transfiguring love of God be known in
the world—known by the way we live and speak
and serve.

People: Amen.

Leader: May the transfiguring grace of Jesus Christ be
shown in us—shown by where and how we live
and work.

People: Amen.

Leader: May the transfiguring power of God's Holy Spirit
guide—guide us in ways of justice, mercy, and
kindness.

People: Amen.

Leader: The peace of the Lord be with you always.

People: And also with you.

Sunday 24

Call to Worship

Leader: You, who delight in the law of the Lord, and who meditate on God's law, day and night, are like trees planted by streams of water.

People: **God's word is a lamp unto our feet, and a light unto our path.**

Leader: The watery grave of your ancestors yields fruit in due season, when justice has prevailed.

People: **Our leaves do not wither. Christ is risen!**

Opening Prayer

Gracious and holy God,
 we give you thanks for your boundless,
 lavishly forgiving love.
We are not worthy to come into your presence,
 but your grace makes us worthy.
We pour out our hearts to you
 like the woman pouring costly perfume
 from the alabaster jar.

We bow before you, as she did, with hearts overflowing with gratitude and love. Amen.

Prayer of Confession

We have strayed, O God,
from your will and your way.
Like the brothers of Joseph,
we have betrayed family and friends
for our own vainglory;
we have enslaved others
to suit our purposes;
we have lied
to cover our tracks;
we have forgotten our faith
when it is convenient;
we have failed you and each other
so many times.
Heal us, O God. Amen.

Words of Assurance

God loves us with a deep and abiding love. God's promises are sure. They shall not hurt or destroy on all God's holy mountains.

Unison Prayer

Lord, we come this morning
seeking to abide in your presence.

Open our minds to your spirit of wisdom,
   that we may know how to live as your people.
Open our hearts to your spirit of truth,
   that we may love all your people with a love
      that speaks of justice, kindness,
         and radical grace.
May this time of worship
   be authentic and pleasing to you. Amen.

Benediction

Leader: God calls us, just as God called the three disciples on the mountaintop, to listen to God's Chosen One, Jesus.

People: With God's help, we will open our minds and hearts and ears to Christ.

Leader: Christ calls us to behold the glory of God's kingdom, made known in prayer.

People: May we, in our praying, be filled with the brightness of God's glory, that through us, God's glory may become real to those in need.

Leader: God's transforming love go with you.

People: **And with you also.**

Leader: The richness of the grace of Jesus Christ abide in you.

People: **And also in you.**

Leader: The renewing power of the Holy Spirit sustain you in your daily service.

People: **And you also. Amen.**

Sunday 25

Call to Worship

Leader: Blessed are you who hunger. Come and be filled.

People: **We come, hungering for justice and righteous-ness.**

Leader: Blessed are you who weep. Come and be comforted.

People: **We come, seeking joy and laughter.**

Leader: Blessed are you who suffer for Christ. Come and be Christ's chosen ones.

People: **We come, yearning for strength to persevere.**

Leader: Come, the worship of God is our joy and our strength.

Opening Prayer

Wondrous Spirit, we come into your holy presence
knowing that you receive us gladly and eagerly.
Morning by morning, you listen for us,
and morning by morning our hearts leap up to you.
Grace our lives with your presence this day.

Hold us in your hands, lead us in your ways,
  and keep us in your love. Amen.

Prayer of Confession

God of Love,
  we have come here today for a family reunion!
We know that we are sisters and brothers in Christ.
Each of us is your precious child.
And yet there is division in this family.
There is sibling rivalry, old resentments, new irritations.
We are quick to anger, slow to forgive.
We would rather choose our relatives,
  than acknowledge the all-inclusive nature
    of your family.
Open our hearts to your love,
  and show us the way of reconciliation.
Teach us to see each brother and sister with your eyes.
Help us claim our heritage as your own children,
  and live together in unity as your family.

Words of Assurance

When we are not sure how to pray,
  or if we are even able to address God in prayer,
  the Spirit intercedes for us
  with sighs too deep for words.
Know that no matter what, nothing,

absolutely nothing can ever separate us
from God's presence and God's love.

Unison Prayer

Holy God, creator of a new reality
   just now coming into view,
      we have come today to see and touch
         and know your presence here among us.
Be with us as we listen for your call.
Help us hear afresh the good news:
that power and steadfast love
   arise from you, our rock and our salvation. Amen.
God of new realities close at hand,
   open our ears to hear your call.
Give us the insight to know that it is you who calls us.
Grant us the courage to go where you send us
   as we journey with the risen Christ. Amen.

Benediction

Go forth, celebrating faith.
Go forth, celebrating hope.
Go forth, celebrating love.
Go forth to be the transformed people
   that God calls us to be.
Go forth to transform the world—
   in times of prosperity,

but most especially, in times of disbelief,
> hostility, fear, and rejection.
Go forth with the knowledge
> that you are always surrounded
> > by the presence of our steadfast, loving God,
> > our rock and our redeemer.

Sunday 26

Call to Worship

People: **We bow down in awe and worship before you.**

Leader: Holy is the Lord!

People: **Let us praise God's great and wondrous name!**

Leader: The Lord's brightness shines upon us.

People: **We will pray and sing in glad thanksgiving to God.**

Leader: The Lord hears and answers the songs and prayers of the faithful.

People: **We will call on God in fervent prayer and praise!**

Leader: Holy is the Lord!

People: **Alleluia!**

Opening Prayer

God of love and healing, you freed us from our chains by revealing the way of faith in Jesus Christ. Through our baptism, you accepted us as your sons and daughters and clothed us in the love of Christ. We welcome your presence

as we lift our lives to you, and open our souls to your renewing Spirit, through Jesus Christ, our Lord. Amen.

Prayer of Confession

Holy God,
>   we come to you
>>   remembering your wonderful miracles,
>>   and fearing your awesome judgment.

We are wholly dependent on your grace
>   and your nurturing faith.

We try, then fail; seek, then forget;
>   hope, then lose sight of your love for us.

Forgive our hesitation, skepticism, and despair.

Help us remove the stumbling blocks
>   placed in our path.

Strengthen us for the journey
>   toward faith, hope, and love,
>>   that we may act for goodness in all we do.

We are your loving children. Amen.

God of fruitful labor,
>   work sometimes brings out the worst in us.

At home, at school, in the workplace,
>   even in our relationship with you,
>>   we too easily question what others do and get,
>>   instead of taking care of our own business.

Take away our bitterness.

Teach us the art of the careful complaint.
Give us grateful hearts, we pray. Amen.

Words of Assurance

God loves us with an unending, steadfast love.
Because of this love,
    God turns away from anger to forgiveness.
Rejoice and be glad in this promise and this reality.

Unison Prayer

May our hearts be open to these words of grace.
May we see with new eyes
    and hear with enlivened ears
        the call to live our lives in accordance
        with the Spirit who gives us new birth. Amen.

Benediction

Live as God's people,
    through the power of the Holy Spirit.
Hold firm to the word preached to you,
    through the grace of the risen Lord.
Lift up your hands and hearts
    and receive God's blessing.
In the name of the Father, and the Son,
    and the Holy Spirit,
        go forth to share the truth of the gospel
            to a watching world.

Sunday 27

Call to Worship

Leader: With heavy burdens we come to you.

People: We have seen a great light!

Leader: Out of darkness we come seeking you, O Lord.

People: We have seen a great light!

Leader: You are our light and our salvation.

People: We have seen a great light!

Leader: We have no fear in the strength of your shelter.

People: We have seen a great light!

Leader: God's kingdom is near!

People: We have seen a great light! Amen!

Opening Prayer

O God who never changes, we come before you on this day, to seek the change that only you can bring to our wounded hearts and broken spirits. From the bumps and bruises we receive through daily living, we come to this place and time to be transformed, cleansed, and healed. O Lord who was and is and is to come, give us faith to become more fully the reflections of your love you have called us to become. Breathe on us the Breath of transforming life, the Holy Spirit of Christ Jesus. We gather in anticipation of your work in our lives. Amen.

Prayer of Confession

God of patience,
   your people grow weary.
We complain and question.
We put you to the test.
Our mouths say yes,
   but our deeds say no.
When we wander off your path,
   when we fail to follow through on our good intentions,
   when we give our attention to trivial things;
      gently call us back to you.
Empty our hearts of anger and pride.
Empty our souls of greed and selfishness.
Empty our minds of envy, doubt, and mistrust.
As you poured out your very self
   through your beloved Son,
   pour your Spirit into our hearts today.
Forgive us our wrongdoing.
Reclaim us with your love.

Words of Assurance

The God who has made us will never desert us.
The God of creation is creating still, making us new.

The God whose love gave us the gift of Jesus Christ
is the same God whose love forgives and sustains us.
Amen.

Unison Prayer

Powerful, compassionate giver of mystery,
grant us the courage to say "yes"
to your unexpected call,
and the strength to claim our place with Christ
in the new creation you are cultivating. Amen.

Benediction

Go forth into the world as people reborn.
Live generosity, not greed.
Celebrate life, not death.
Revel in the abundant grace
that flows over and through us,
and bring that love and grace
to a world deeply in need.
Go in peace. Amen.

Sunday 28

Call to Worship

Leader: We come to worship you Lord, seeking refuge from doubt and freedom from fear.

People: We yearn to live in the shelter of your presence.

Leader: Lord, you break the bonds of our oppression with the piercing clarity of your light.

People: You lift our burdens, surrounding us with hope.

Leader: Let those who have experienced darkness feel the promise of your eternal radiance.

People: We shout for joy, secure in the knowledge of your love. Amen!

Opening Prayer

O Lord God of freedom, we gather for worship and direction. Chains and walls and locks and burdens hinder our knowing freedom in your Spirit. Come to us now, as we come to you. Help us to know how to find release from those physical and mental prisons we have established in the midst of our fear and doubt. Open the gates of our minds and hearts, and invite us into a discipleship that is both delightful and demanding. Send us out encouraged, enthused, and empowered, with the energy and Spirit of Pentecost, when tongues of fire descended upon your people. Amen.

Prayer of Confession

God of mercy,
  in our impatience for answers,
  we sometimes turn to idols of our own making
      and forget our covenant with you.
Passionate for what is right,
  we wrong those with whom we differ.
Pleased at the invitation to your banquet,
  we fail to arrive with humility and thanksgiving.
Forgive us when our faith is weak
  and our zeal too strong.
In Jesus' name we pray. Amen.

Words of Assurance

Hear the words of the Lord:
  "I will make a way in the wilderness
      and rivers in the desert.
For I give water in the wilderness,
  rivers in the desert, to give drink
      to my chosen people.

I, I am He who blots out your transgressions
   for my own sake,
     and I will not remember your sins."
The dust has been swept away. The walk is clear.
People of the covenant, your life in Christ awaits you.
   God's grace is sufficient. Amen.

Unison Prayer

Lord, from emptiness, you create substance—
   when we hunger,
      you fill us from your abundance;
   when all seems lost,
      you bring hope and salvation,
      you make possible the impossible.
We are overcome with joy,
   but we are also terrified of your power.
Calm and strengthen our hearts
   as we hear your assurance,
      "It is I: Do not be afraid." Amen.

Benediction

May the transforming love of God
   work in your lives, today and always.
Go forth into the world with peace, love, and joy.
Follow Christ wherever he leads you.
Fulfill the promise found in the fruit of the Spirit. Amen.

Sunday 29

Call to Worship

Leader: The LORD is Sovereign.

People: Let the people tremble in awe.

Leader: God is enthroned between the cherubim.

People: Let the earth shake.

Leader: The LORD is great in Zion.

People: God is high above all peoples. Come let us worship our glorious Lord.

Opening Prayer

Almighty Lord, Faithful Friend, your Word begs to be heard. It pleads for us to respond. And yet we do nothing. The pain of a wounded person is ignored. The plight of a hungry child is dismissed. Touch our hearts, O patient Healer. Compel us to respond with compassion, as you have responded to us. Heal us of our callous and cold hearts, and open our eyes and hearts to the needs around us. Dwell within us, that we may bring hope and healing to the last, the lost, and to those considered to be least around the earth. Amen.

Prayer of Confession

O God,
    we lead busy lives.
Just coming to church on Sunday mornings
    often seems like a sacrifice.
There's so much to do,
    so much to worry about.
We read about being an olive tree
    planted in your house, green and flourishing,
        under the care of your presence.
Yet, our roots feel planted most anywhere else:
    in our duties; in our business relationships;
    in our family plans; in our volunteer commitments;
    in our efforts to make it in this world.
When we forget who we are,
    when the soil of our lives becomes barren,
    plant our roots in your goodness and wisdom,
        that we may welcome you into our lives. Amen.

Words of Assurance

In Christ, our release has been secured
    through the shedding of his blood.

Through Jesus, we've been given clean hands
    and pure hearts.
In him, we've received the Lord's blessing.
We've received vindication
    from the God of our salvation.
This is the inheritance of redemption
    for all who seek the Lord,
    and for all who seek the face of God.

Unison Prayer

Holy God,
    you care for our needs
            with your compassionate presence
                    and teachings.
Holy God,
    be our Guest,
        accept our seeking presence,
                and bless us with understanding. Amen.

Benediction

Do not grow weary in doing what is right,
    for you will reap a great harvest
        if you do not give up.
Sow in the Spirit
    and reap the blessings of God.
Go in peace.

Sunday 30

Call to Worship

Leader: God, you call each of us to serve you, and we answer,

People: "Here I am!"

Leader: Jesus, you call each of us to follow you, and we answer,

People: "Here I am!"

Leader: Holy Spirit, you call each of us to worship you this day, and we answer,

People: "Here I am!"

Opening Prayer

What is your will, O God? What plans do you have for us? We strain to hear your whispers, hoping to glean a little understanding. We examine your Word, hoping to unearth a precious verse that might shed light on your intentions. We fervently pray, eager that your will can be revealed to us. But your gentle whispers are drowned out by the hubbub of our lives. Quiet our spirits, O God, that we might discover your will. May the psalmist's plea to "rescue the weak and needy" challenge us to respond. We ask this in the name of the One who taught us to love our neighbors as ourselves. Amen.

Prayer of Confession

God of Mystery,
>we want to stay awake
>>and be ready for your surprises,
>>but we are tired and overcome
>>>with the usual routine.

We want to wait patiently
>for the fulfillment of your kingdom,
>but we are frustrated by our need
>>for immediate gratification.

We want to believe your promises from ancient days,
>but we are overwhelmed with postmodern doubts.

Come to us again, O God.
Awaken us with your unexpected grace.
Shock us with your daring mercy.
Lift us up from lethargy
>and set our feet on your path once more.

(*Prayer continues in silence.*)

Words of Assurance

You were far away.
But by the blood of Christ,

you have been brought near.
In him, you are reconciled to God in one body,
　　as members of the Lord's household.
In Christ, there is peace—
　　peace to you who were faraway;
　　peace to you who have been brought near!

Unison Prayer

Nourishing Parent of all who hunger,
　　thank you for opening our hearts and minds
　　　　to the gift of your word, the bread of heaven.
Help us hunger for your peace and righteousness
　　over the things of this world. Amen.

Benediction

Leader:　We leave the house of God,
People:　but not the presence of God.
Leader:　Let us root ourselves deeply in God's holy presence
People:　and live out God's love for all.
Leader:　Trust in the steadfast love of God forever and ever.

CPSIA information can be obtained at www.ICGtesting.com
Printed in the USA
LVOW131846111012

302462LV00002B/3/P

9 781426 754784